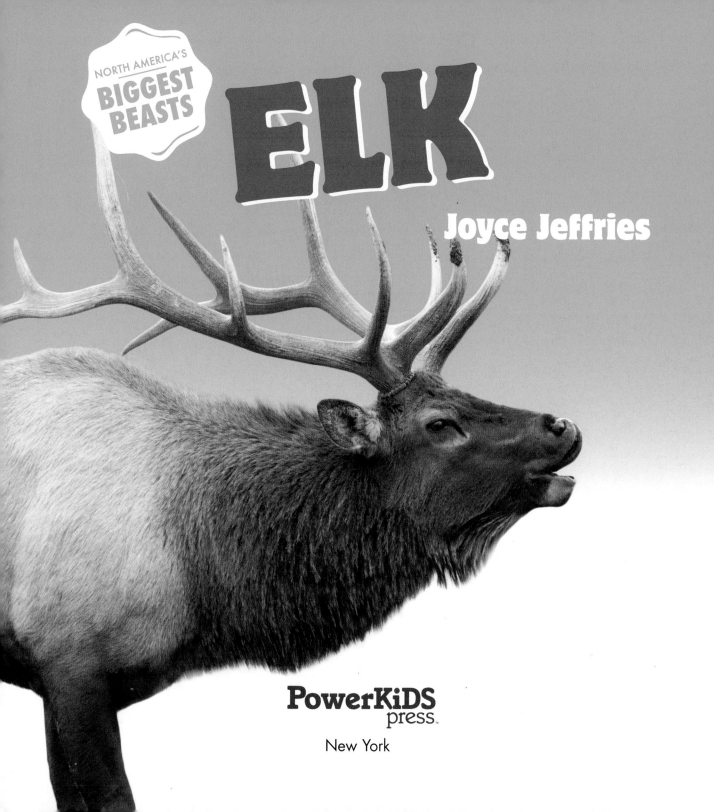

NORTH AMERICA'S
BIGGEST BEASTS

ELK

Joyce Jeffries

PowerKiDS
press.

New York

Published in 2016 by The Rosen Publishing Group, Inc.
29 East 21st Street, New York, NY 10010

First Edition

Editor: Katie Kawa
Book Design: Reann Nye

Photo Credits: Cover (background) BGSmith/Shutterstock.com; cover (elk), p. 1 Danita Delimont/Gallo Images/Getty Images; pp. 4, 8 Tom Reichner/Shutterstock.com; p. 5 Jill Lang/Shutterstock.com; pp. 6–7 (background) cdrin/Shutterstock.com; p. 7 (map) boreala/Shutterstock.com; p. 9 IrinaK/Shutterstock.com; p. 10 Rafa Irusta/Shutterstock.com; p. 11 Kurt M/Shutterstock.com; pp. 12, 15 Travelmages/Shutterstock.com; p. 13 Teri Virbickis/Shutterstock.com; p. 14 (sheep) Eric Isselee/Shutterstock.com; p. 14 (cow) DnD-Production.com/Shutterstock.com; pp. 16 (grizzly bear), 22 Dennis W. Donohue/Shutterstock.com; p. 16 (mountain lion) visceralimage/Shutterstock.com; p. 17 IPK Photography/Shutterstock.com; p. 18 Nathan Chor/Shutterstock.com; p. 19 Images by Dr. Alan Lipkin/Shutterstock.com; p. 20 Julie Lubick/Shutterstock.com; p. 21 Condor 36/Shutterstock.com.

Cataloging-in-Publication Data

Jeffries, Joyce.
Elk / by Joyce Jeffries.
p. cm. — (North America's biggest beasts)
Includes index.
ISBN 978-1-5081-4298-0 (pbk.)
ISBN 978-1-5081-4287-4 (6-pack)
ISBN 978-1-5081-4292-8 (library binding)
1. Elk — Juvenile literature. I. Jeffries, Joyce. II. Title.
QL737.U55 J44 2016
599.65'42—d23

Manufactured in the United States of America

CPSIA Compliance Information: Batch #BW16PK: For Further Information contact Rosen Publishing, New York, New York at 1-800-237-9932

CONTENTS

A Big Deer 4

Where Do Elk Live? 6

A Deer of Different Colors 8

Bulls, Cows, and Calves 10

Moving for Food 12

Chewing Cud 14

Hunting Elk 16

Protecting Elk Populations 18

Sights and Sounds 20

Amazing Animals 22

Glossary 23

Index 24

Websites 24

A Big Deer

Have you ever seen a deer in your backyard or in a park? In some places in North America, you might see a kind of deer that can weigh over 1,000 pounds (453.6 kg)! This huge deer is an elk, which is the largest kind of red deer found in North America.

Elk can stand as tall as 5 feet (1.5 m) at the shoulder. Male elk have large **antlers** that make them even taller. Read on to find out more about these massive **mammals**!

white-tailed deer

THE BIG IDEA

Elk are much larger than the white-tailed deer often seen in North American neighborhoods.

Male elk are generally larger than females. In fact, some males can weigh twice as much as females!

5

Where Do Elk Live?

Elk once had the largest **range** of any species, or kind, of deer in North America. However, overhunting and the loss of their **habitat** led to decreases in their population and range size. Now, North American elk live mainly in the western part of the United States and Canada. However, in the 1900s, elk were reintroduced into some eastern parts of North America, such as Pennsylvania.

Elk can live in many different habitats. They're found on prairies, in valleys, and in **coniferous forests**. They can also be found in the mountains.

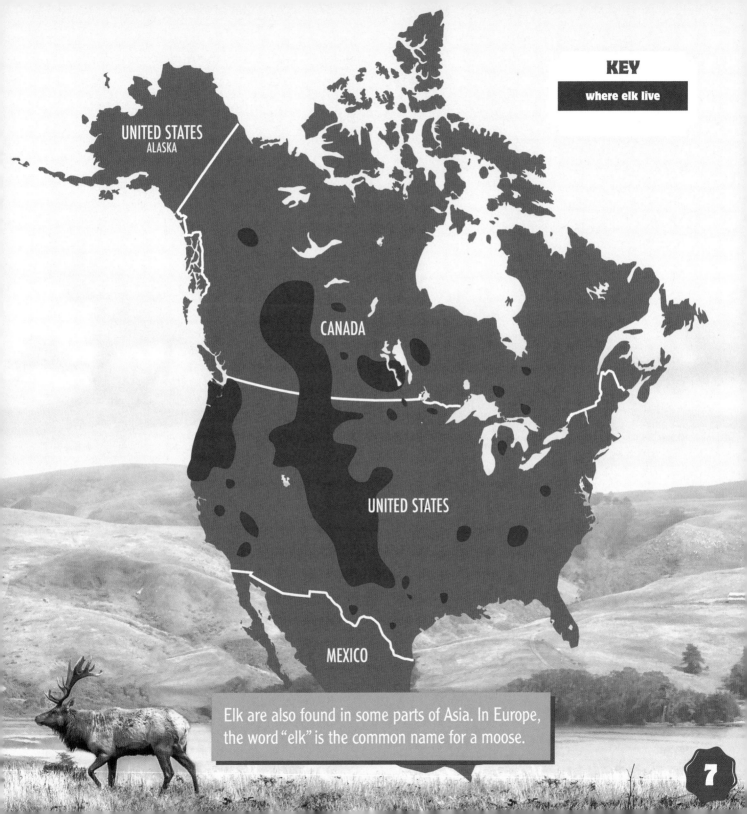

where elk live

UNITED STATES
ALASKA

CANADA

UNITED STATES

MEXICO

Elk are also found in some parts of Asia. In Europe, the word "elk" is the common name for a moose.

A Deer of Different Colors

Elk often live in places where it gets very cold. During the winter, elk grow a dark, shaggy mane of fur on their neck and chest. This mane stands out against the rest of the elk's fur, which is lighter brown or tan. Elk are sometimes called wapiti, which is a Native American word that refers to their light-colored **rump**.

Male elk are also known for their large antlers. These antlers are covered with a soft skin called velvet as they grow. The velvet comes off in time for the **mating** season.

The head, neck, underside, and legs of an elk are darker than the rest of the animal.

Bulls, Cows, and Calves

Mating season for elk is also known as the rut, and it generally takes place in the fall. Male elk use their antlers to fight over female elk. Larger and older males with larger antlers have groups of female elk they mate with. These groups are called harems.

About eight to nine months after the mating season, a female elk gives birth to one baby, or calf. Female elk **protect** their calves after they're born. Males don't play a part in raising calves.

THE BIG IDEA

Male elk are called bulls. Females are called cows.

A newborn elk calf can weigh as much as 35 pounds (16 kg)! Calves can stand on their own minutes after they're born.

Moving for Food

   Elk calves drink milk from their mother after they're born, but they soon start to eat grasses, too. Grasses and flowering plants, such as violets, are among an elk's favorite foods. During the summer, elk eat these plants at higher **elevations**. When the weather gets colder, elk migrate, or travel, to lower elevations where it's easier to find food.

   In the winter, elk often have to dig through snow to find grasses. They also eat **shrubs** and branches from trees. Elk are herbivores, which means they only eat plants.

Elk need to eat a large amount of food every day because they're such big animals.

Chewing Cud

Elk are ruminant animals. This means they chew their food only enough to swallow it at first. Then, the food is stored in a chamber, or part, of the elk's stomach called the rumen. Eventually, the chewed food in the rumen is brought back up to the elk's mouth, where it's chewed again to help the elk break down the food.

After the elk finishes chewing its cud, or the food it already swallowed once, the food goes back into the stomach. An elk's stomach has four chambers!

sheep

cow

THE BIG IDEA

Other ruminant animals include cows and sheep.

Chewing cud helps an elk get as many **nutrients** as possible from the plants it eats.

Hunting Elk

Although an elk's large size makes it hard for another animal to attack it, elk are still hunted by some big predators. Wolf packs and mountain lions eat elk. Bears, such as grizzly bears and American black bears, hunt elk, too. Bobcats and coyotes are known to eat elk calves.

People also hunt elk for food and for sport. In fact, hunting is one of the main reasons why elk are no longer seen in most of the eastern United States.

mountain lion

grizzly bear

THE BIG IDEA

Elk can run quickly for being such large animals. They can run at speeds of up to 35 miles (56.3 km) per hour!

Elk use their speed and strong senses of sight, hearing, and smell to avoid predators.

Protecting Elk Populations

People can legally hunt elk in the United States in limited numbers, but hunting laws differ by state and season. It's important to follow those laws if you ever go hunting with an adult.

Elk also suffered from the loss of their habitats as people began building across North America. Protected lands such as national parks have helped elk populations for many years. Yellowstone National Park is home to many elk. Wyoming's National Elk Refuge is another protected place for elk to live.

These elk have found a home at the National Elk Refuge in Wyoming. A refuge is a place that provides protection for animals.

Sights and Sounds

If you want to see an elk, there are signs to look and listen for that will tell you if an elk's been in the area. Because elk are so heavy, they leave hoof prints, which are also called tracks, on almost any surface—from snow to mud. Elk also leave **depressions** in the ground called wallows. Trees and shrubs sometimes have marks on them from an elk's antlers.

Elk are the loudest deer in North America! Males are known for bugling, or making a deep roaring sound.

THE BIG IDEA

Elk are seen most often in early morning and late evening.

ELK SIGNS

NAME	WHAT IS IT?	WHAT CAUSES IT?
bugle	low, loud roaring sound	Males make this sound to find a mate.
track	hoof print on the ground—looks like a split heart and is 4 inches (10.2 cm) long and 3 inches (7.6 cm) wide	Elk are so heavy they leave hoof prints wherever they walk.
wallow	deep depression in the ground with elk fur on the bottom and hoof prints around it	Elk roll in the mud to find a mate, to get rid of bugs, or to lose their winter coat.
rub	trees with missing bark and plants with missing leaves or branches	Male elk rub their antlers on shrubs and trees to get the velvet off.

If you see or hear any of these signs, an elk was probably in your area not long ago!

Amazing Animals

Elk are amazing animals. They have strong senses, speedy legs, and big bodies. They travel far each year to find food in both winter and summer. They also provide food for other animals, including people.

It's important to protect elk because their populations have already decreased so much due to people's actions. Elk hunters should always follow the correct hunting laws. If we do our part, herds of elk will be walking across parts of North America for many years to come.

Glossary

antler: One of the bony horns on a deer.

coniferous forest: A forest of trees that produce cones, such as pine trees.

depression: A flattened area of land where the center is lower than the land around it.

elevation: Height above sea level.

habitat: The natural home for plants, animals, and other living things.

mammal: Any warm-blooded animal whose babies drink milk and whose body is covered with hair or fur.

mate: To come together to make babies. Also, one of two animals that come together to make babies.

nutrient: Something taken in by a plant or animal that helps it grow and stay healthy.

protect: To keep safe.

range: An open area of land over which animals move and feed.

rump: The back part of an animal's body where the thighs join the hips.

shrub: A low, woody plant.

Index

A
antlers, 4, 8, 10,
    20, 21

B
bugle, 20, 21

C
calves, 10, 11,
    12, 16
Canada, 6
cud, 14, 15

D
deer, 4, 6, 20

F
females, 5, 10
food, 12, 13, 14,
    16, 22
fur, 8, 21

H
habitat, 6, 18
harems, 10
herbivores, 12
hunting, 16, 18, 22

L
laws, 18, 22

M
males, 4, 5, 8, 10,
    20, 21
mammals, 4
mane, 8
mating season,
    8, 10

N
National Elk Refuge,
    18, 19

P
predators, 16, 17

R
rub, 21
rumen, 14
ruminant animals, 14
rut, 10

S
species, 6

T
tracks, 20, 21

U
United States, 6,
    16, 18

V
velvet, 8, 21

W
wallows, 20, 21
wapiti, 8

Y
Yellowstone National
    Park, 18

Websites

Due to the changing nature of Internet links, PowerKids Press has developed an
online list of websites related to the subject of this book. This site is updated regularly.
Please use this link to access the list: www.powerkidslinks.com/nabb/elk